# A Table Before Me



PAULINE ELLIS CRAMER

**Pacific Press Publishing Association**
Boise, Idaho
Oshawa, Ontario, Canada

Unless otherwise indicated, Scripture references in this book are from the New International Version.

Edited by Bonnie Widicker
Designed by Dennis Ferree
Cover by Marlene Hintz
Typeset in 12/13 Adobe Garamond



Library of Congress Cataloging-in-Publication Data:
Cramer, Pauline Ellis.
A table before me: devotions for overeaters who crave the power of God / Pauline Ellis Cramer.
p. cm.
ISBN 0-8163-1079-3
1. Eating disorders—Patients—Prayer-books and devotions—English. I. Title.
BV4910.35.C73 1992
242'.4—dc20 91-38002
CIP

92 93 94 95 96 • 5 4 3 2

*To my husband, Judd, who*
*has loved me through*
*thick and thin.*
*AND*
*To my children,*
*Juddaca and Jim.*
*Their faith in me*
*nourished my perseverance.*

# *SPRING STORM*

***Be my rock of refuge, to which I can always go; give the command to save me, for you are my rock and my fortress (Psalm 71:3).***

My niece, Andrea, helps us with the cattle when she's not attending college. One spring day she rode high into the mountains to check the cows and calves. The blue skies that morning convinced her to wear only a light jacket, but she tied her waterproof duster behind her saddle.

For four hours, her horse carried her into the desolate areas of the mountain. Wisps of grass, sagebrush, and rocks stretched for miles in all directions. She hoped to locate the cows by early afternoon, check whether they had good feed and adequate water, then return home before dark.

As she rode higher and higher, the air became cooler. Behind her, the sky changed from blue to black. Then, without warning, the storm broke. Andrea had only enough time to dismount next to a large boulder and make a tent with her duster. As the wind whirled the sleet and snow around her, she crouched next to the rock, clutching the horse's reins. For twenty minutes the snow and ice cut her off completely from the rest of the world. All she could see was the boulder and her horse's silhouette.

As quickly as the storm came, it left. Andrea watched the black clouds roll over the next mountain peak, leaving innocent blue skies in its trail. Birds began flying again, the horse shook the ice from his mane, and the sun began to melt the snow. Within minutes, the world transformed from winter back to spring. Andrea rode on, wondering whether the storm had been real or merely a dream.

Determining reality is even more difficult at times for me. I react with unrealistic fear to the storms of life. I deal with them by either denying or avoiding them. I overeat in an effort to hide from the storm or for comfort from it.

But food doesn't shelter me; it adds to my pain.

Today, I turned to God instead of to food for refuge from a storm in my life. He protected me from the turmoil and gave me victory over fear.

## *Prayer*

***I lift my voice in praise of my God. He is my rock in whom I take refuge (see Psalm 18:2).***

## Affirmation

God is my sheltering rock from the storms of life.

# *ALL OUR CARES*

***Cast all your anxiety on him because he cares for you (1 Peter 5:7 ).***

I dug through five moving crates before locating the thermometer and alcohol. While I took my infant son's temperature, I searched the Yellow Pages for a pediatrician. Then I swabbed the thermometer with alcohol and popped it into my five-year-old daughter's mouth. I dialed seven doctors before I found one who took new patients, immediately. While rummaging through more boxes for an umbrella, I tried to convince myself a 102° temperature wasn't a panic situation.

Hugging my infant son to me in one arm and carrying my daughter in the other, I raced through the deluge for our car. After shaking the raindrops from my hair, I studied a city map.

We drove through torrents of rain for thirty minutes before I realized I was hopelessly lost. Both kids were crying in hoarse voices when the car died.

"Lord, please help!" I wept.

"Mommy, can God take care of this much trouble?"

"Sure, honey."

Her question was the same one I once asked a friend back in Baton Rouge. She told me, "When the devil throws me a flaming ball of trouble, I just hit it like a volleyball and say, 'Lord, take care of this, thank Ya kindly.' "

"I'm hurling this one on to you, Lord . . ." The sound of tapping on my side window interrupted my prayer.

"Do you need help?" a woman asked.

She drove us the three blocks to the doctor and brought gasoline to my car. I never saw the woman (or angel) again, but I know who sent her.

Peter told us to "cast *all* our anxiety on God," not merely the big problems. Sometimes I feel that being overweight is a big problem only to me. God has more important things to deal with. If I believe Peter, and I do, then such thoughts limit God's caring for me.

## *Prayer*

***Lord, help me lose weight.***

## Affirmation

Thanks, Lord.

# *PRIORITIES*

***Do not set your heart on what you will eat or drink; do not worry about it. For the pagan world runs after all such things, and your Father knows that you need them. But seek his kingdom, and these things will be given to you as well (Luke 12:29-31).***

My husband and I married in our teens. Those early years of marriage were difficult financially. Because my husband had a full scholarship, he was able to finish his college education. I worked as a secretary to earn needed income.

During the five years I worked, a deep dissatisfaction constantly gnawed at me. I felt that if we could afford another child, I would be fulfilled.

After my husband graduated, our second child was born. By his first birthday, the routine of diapers, feedings, and story times left a painful void inside once again. I became convinced that I needed the intellectual stimulation of college classes.

The classes helped but didn't provide total satisfaction. Then I kept reassuring myself that the answer would come when I began my teaching career.

A loving husband, children, college degree, career, and a bright future—what more could I possibly need? The void within grew more apparent with each external accomplishment. What could I do to find inner peace?

I had been ignoring a basic principle of Christianity that I had been taught. Seek God first. When I finally started each day with devotions and thanked God throughout the day for each good thing, the void filled with serenity. When I asked for His guidance in every decision, whether large or small, my blessings and accomplishments became a joy.

Overeating is a matter of the heart as well as the mind. It's the futile search for satisfaction through food. I must remember to put God first in all phases of my life, or my hunger will never be satisfied. Seeking His kingdom, I will find *lasting* satisfaction.

***Lord, I need to be reminded often to put You first.***

## Affirmation

I seek His kingdom first.

# *ARMOR*

***I want to remind you that your strength must come from the Lord's mighty power within you. Put on all of God's armor so that you will be able to stand safe against all strategies and tricks of Satan (Ephesians 6:10, 11, TLB).***

This morning when I dressed for the women's meeting, I put on some different accessories. First, I buckled on the "belt of truth." *Lord, help me guard against telling myself lies. You and I both know I don't need a "shot of sugar" at the midmorning break. Help me choose a bagel in place of a doughnut.*

Next, I protected my heart and emotions with the "breastplate of God's approval." *You know, Lord, there will be several women at this meeting with slender figures. Help me overcome discouragement with my excess weight when I see them. Protect me from trying to comfort my feelings with food. Help me accept Your approval of me.*

I then slipped on the "shoes of readiness." *Lord, I can race past the luncheon dishes covered with cream sauces if You strengthen my steps. Help me march right up to the salads and fill my plate.*

Before I went out the door, I grabbed the "shield of faith" and the "hat of salvation." I felt confident the Lord would protect me from the arrows of doubt and fear. God was saving me from old, negative habits and behavior patterns.

The last accessory I added, before I left my car for the conference room, was prayer.

God brought me a friend to visit with during the midmorning break. Nourished by companionship, I even forgot about the bagel.

Before entering the lunchroom, I breathed a short prayer for strength. Filled with God's peace, I made one stop at the salad table and was satisfied. The Lord shielded me from the creamed casseroles and the desserts.

It was a victorious day. I knew without a doubt that my strength came from the "Lord's mighty power" within me.

***Lord, thank You for helping me to remain alert and to keep on praying (see Ephesians 6:18).***

## Affirmation

Through God's power, I am victorious.

# A CHILD'S FAITH

***I tell you the truth, anyone who will not receive the kingdom of God like a little child will never enter it (Luke 18:17).***

I loved watching my second graders enter the class room on the first day of school. After a barefoot summer, they walked gingerly in shoes that pinched. Their stiff, new jeans swished as they moved about. Many suntanned faces were crowned with golden hair, bleached from playing in the summer sun. Some children beamed bright, open smiles; others carried smiles with trembling lips. All wiggled and giggled with part fear and part exhilaration.

After the final bell rang, they sat at their desks, expectantly waiting for me to speak.

Standing in front of my desk, I offered them my brightest smile and said in my friendliest voice, "You are all lucky. I'm a nice teacher."

In unison they released long sighs and whispered to each other, "O-o-oh good!"

"In second grade," I continued, "we have a lot of exciting things to learn, such as how to tell time and write in cursive. When we learn new things, we sometimes make mistakes. That's OK. That's part of learning. I'll be here to help you."

At morning recess I overheard some of my students tell their friends, "Our teacher's nice."

"How do you know already?"

"She told us."

"You're so lucky!"

"We know. She told us that too."

I'm lucky, also. I have a nice God. He told me in the Scriptures. He lovingly helps me with my mistakes when I confess them. Whether I'm striving to become a better Christian witness or merely trying to improve my eating habits, the Holy Spirit is there to help and guide me.

## Prayer

***Father, help me to have a child's pure faith in You.***

## Affirmation

I have a nice God.

# *GARDEN OF EDEN*

***The Lord God had planted a garden in the east, in Eden; and there he put the man he had formed (Genesis 2:8).***

One of my great pleasures in life is my small herb-and-flower garden. The circular bed has an inner circle filled with multicolored strawflowers. Eight pie-shaped beds—each with its own theme—radiate out from the center circle. One I call my salad bowl. In it I grow lettuce, green onions, radishes, spinach, cabbage, and parsley. Next to my salad bowl is my Shakespearean bed. Each flower and herb in this bed is mentioned in one of Shakespeare's plays.

Other beds have themes of Bible plants, fragrance, herbal teas, cooking herbs, and cheerfulness. The last one is my favorite. It's my showcase for giant Oriental poppies and brilliant gloriosa daisies. Their vivid colors rarely fail to lift my spirits.

My tiny Garden of Eden didn't appear in our backyard one day merely by wishful thinking. I planned, prepared, and planted it. Daily, I water and weed it. I seek expert advice about its care and nurturing. I also admit, I talk to my plants.

When life become chaotic, I love to sit on a bench in my garden to absorb its tranquility. Its geometric shape gives me a feeling of stability. The presence of bees, butterflies, and ladybugs assures me of God's plan for harmony in nature. Its cycles of growth and predictable changes remind me of God's divine order.

As I lingered in my garden this morning, I found a lesson for my day. God controls the harmony in nature and *offers* harmony in my life. All I need do is turn the control over to Him. *God, I release control of my life to You, including my compulsive overeating. Help me nurture the cycle of growth within me.*

I turned my gaze to my cheerfulness flower bed. The poppies and daisies whispered to me, "You are more beautiful to God than we are to you."

## Prayer

***Is it true, Lord? Am I as lovely to You as the flowers are to me? I praise Your name for giving me and nature the beauty of Your harmony.***

## Affirmation

"A great burden falls away if we let God run the universe" (Robert Cummings).

# *JACOB'S STAIRWAY*

***Jacob left Beersheba and set out for Haran. When he reached a certain place, he stopped for the night . . . and lay down to sleep. He had a dream in which he saw a stairway resting on the earth, with its top reaching to heaven, and the angels of God were ascending and descending on it (Genesis 28:10-12).***

When I was a child, I loved to look at the colored pictures in my mother's Bible. My favorite picture showed a stairway beginning on earth and rising into the clouds of heaven. It depicted an angel talking to Jacob and pointing up the stairs. Jacob stood at the bottom, looking upward.

I gazed at the picture, thinking that if I were Jacob, I would race up those stairs. I had a million questions I wanted to ask God. How could Jacob stand there, peering up at such an opportunity, and not climb toward it?

Only a child, with an innocent heart, would *race* into God's presence. As an adult, like Jacob, I've often found myself merely gazing up the stairs.

I've discovered four different stairways to a closer relationship with God. One stairway is the intellectual. To climb this one, I study the Scriptures and Christian writings. I go to church and Bible studies to challenge my mind toward continuous growth.

Another stairway is the emotional. To ascend this one, I need to drop off bundles on each step. On the first step, I might lay down anger and hurt feelings. The next one could be fear, followed by resentments or guilt.

A third stairway is the spiritual. I gain access to each upward step through prayer and meditation. I open my heart and my mind to the Holy Spirit.

I've barely begun to understand the physical stairway. As an overeater, this is an important climb for me. The first step I took was turning my food abuse over to God's control. The next step was joining a support group like Overeaters Anonymous. The third step was the most frightening and most rewarding—abstinence. I now abstain from sweets and snacks. I eat three meals a day and no more.

By choosing to take these steps toward God, He has met me more than halfway. He gives me the courage and strength to keep climbing.

## *Prayer*

***Thank You, Lord, for showing me the stairways toward a closer relationship with You.***

## Affirmation

I'm climbing the stairway of victory.

# *POCKETS*

***Where your treasure is, there your heart will be also (Luke 12:34).***

When my son was two years old, I bought him a pair of Osh-Kosh overalls. It was love at first wearing. The numerous pockets were exactly what he needed. From that day on, if his Osh-Kosh overalls were anywhere to be found, that's what he wanted to wear that day. It didn't matter to him whether he was playing outside or going to church.

When I laundered his overalls, emptying the pockets became a treasure hunt. Each pocket contained at least one object. He collected plastic-bag twisters, metal washers, soda-can tabs, assorted rocks, and rubber bands.

One day in my haste, I forgot to empty his pockets before throwing the overalls into the washer. Later, when I opened the washing machine to add the fabric softener, six dead crickets floated on the top of the rinse water. After I recovered from the shock, I began to worry that I had destroyed his prize crickets. Would he remember and ask me about them?

As I scooped the crickets out of the rinse water, I chuckled to myself, thinking, *To my little one, these are as valuable as diamonds and emeralds. He carries his precious possessions in his pocket.* I found a paper towel and laid the six crickets on it to dry.

If I could carry my greatest treasures in my pocket, what would I put there? Like my son's treasures, they wouldn't be gems of great value. They would be gifts from God such as my growing personal relationship with Jesus Christ; my family's love; and my good health. Another jewel I hunt for, to put in my pocket, is victory over compulsive eating.

I know God wants to fill my pockets with this victory; but I stuff them full of trash, such as anger, resentments, lack of faith, and anxiety. I must willingly open my pockets, clean out the garbage, and make room for God to fill them with His blessings.

## Prayer

***Heavenly Father, I thank You for the blessings You've poured into some of my pockets. As I empty the rubbish from other pockets, I see You filling them with victory over food addiction.***

## Affirmation

"There are good things God must delay giving, until his child has a pocket to hold them" (George MacDonald).

# FEED BAG

***Encourage one another and build each other up, just as in fact you are doing (1 Thessalonians 5:11).***

When I first got my miniature dachshund, Julie, I allowed her in the stables with me while I groomed and saddled Ramboss, my gelding. Julie loved exploring the barn's nooks and crannies while weaving her way around Ramboss's feet. Curious about the little animal, Ramboss kept lowering his head to sniff her, trying to figure out what she was.

When ready to ride, I'd put Julie safely back in our house—and listen to her cries as I rode down our long lane. Her howls haunted me until I came up with a great idea. I bought a horse's feed bag, slipped her into the bag, and hung it from the saddle horn. Only her neck and head extended from the bag. She loved it, and Ramboss seemed pleased with the extra little passenger.

On sunny days, when Ramboss's gait was slow, Julie laid her head against the horse's neck and dozed. If we switched to a gallop, my dachie stretched up her neck to catch the wind, her long ears flapping to the rhythm of the hooves.

One day during a full gallop, the strap of the feed bag snapped. Julie plummeted to the ground. Instantly, Ramboss halted, nearly throwing me over his head. Somehow he knew she had fallen and that one of his steps could crush her.

Luckily, Julie landed in a clump of deep grass. She scooted out of the bag, wobbled over to Ramboss's front legs, and sat down. Ramboss lowered his head to check on her. A 1,200-pound horse and a twelve-pound dog were committed to a lifelong friendship.

How committed am I to my dieting friends? Do I stop to support and encourage them when they fall? By helping another person, I gain a spiritual uplift and a deeper commitment to my own goals.

***Lord, show me ways that I can encourage my friends.***

## Affirmation

I am open and aware to situations where I can help.

# *RATTLER*

***He who trusts in himself is a fool, but he who walks in wisdom is kept safe (Proverbs 28:26).***

One day while hiking in the mountains near my home, I discovered an abandoned, rocky road. With an adventurous spirit, I decided to investigate it. After I had followed it uphill for half a mile, the road turned into a soft dirt path. It continued upward through sweet-smelling pines. The only sound was the tread of my hiking boots and the wind brushing through the tops of the conifers.

At the summit I was surprised to find a secluded, verdant valley below. Part of its treasures was an abandoned homestead with a dilapidated log home and barn. I fell in love with this trail and now walk it two or three times a week.

As I hike, my mind drifts inward with prayers, plans, and praises. I often get so deep in thought, however, that I have developed the habit of gazing at the ground where I step instead of *ahead* of my steps. On one hike, while lost in thought, I almost lowered my foot on a rattlesnake.

Panic is a rapid teacher. I'm now much better at looking ahead as I hike.

Dieting is like watching for rattlers. If I don't watch ahead with my eating plan, I can find myself stepping into danger zones. For example, I know it's best to go to the grocery store soon after a meal. Allowing myself to get too hungry can result in grabbing the first foods available. These are usually high-fat, sugary foods.

Exhaustion is another "rattler" to watch out for. Fatigue makes cleaning fresh vegetables and fruit or preparing a nutritious meal an overwhelming chore.

I will keep cleaned vegetables and fruit available in my refrigerator. I will plan my day's meals ahead and prepare part of them. By providing for my weak times, I won't be as tempted to indulge in panic eating of rich, fattening foods.

## Prayer

***Heavenly Father, help me walk in Your wisdom, not in my foolishness.***

## Affirmation

Wisdom means planning ahead.

# *WOBBLE*

***If you leave God's paths and go astray, you will hear a Voice behind you say, "No, this is the way; walk here" (Isaiah 30:21, TLB).***

At the sound of my one-year-old daughter's scream, I rushed into the kitchen. In her attempt to walk the distance between chairs, she'd taken a tumble. A drop of blood trickled from her lip as I picked her up. I held her tightly to me, cooing comforting words while reaching into the freezer for ice.

I wrapped the ice in a towel and held it to her lip. "I know it hurts, sweetheart, but this will help." Her teary eyes looked at me with doubt, but she allowed me to hold the ice in place. When she calmed down, I examined her lip. There was a slight cut but nothing serious.

A few hours later, her pain forgotten, she once again tried a balancing act between chairs. I knew she would eventually learn to walk. All she needed to do was keep trying. Each bump and fall wasn't failure, but teaching times on how to succeed.

Like my daughter, who was learning to physically walk, I'm learning to walk spiritually. Unlike my daughter, who had to let go of my hand, I must cling to God's hand. He assures me, "I know this hurts a little, but it will help you feel better."

Today, shaking like a toddler struggling from chair to chair, I walked past the candy in the gas station, paid my bill, and walked back out. I wobbled, but I didn't fall. I'm taking steps toward proper nutrition by listening to the Voice of victory whispering behind me, "This is the way; walk here."

## Prayer

***Lord, I listen for Your whispers, and I hear them.***

## Affirmation

I'm learning to walk with success.

# *DAILY LESSONS*

***His divine power has given us everything we need for life and godliness. . . . For this very reason, make every effort to add to your faith goodness; and to goodness, knowledge; and to knowledge, self-control; and to self-control, perseverance; and to perseverance, godliness; and to godliness, brotherly kindness; and to brotherly kindness, love (2 Peter 1:3-7).***

When I became aware of how serious my battle with weight had become, I was terribly despondent. I prayed, in faith, for God to take away my addiction. He led me to seek knowledge about my problem and how to overcome it. At times the amount of information about dieting and food addiction overwhelmed and confused me. I asked God for wisdom. He whispered, "Draw closer to Me." I've learned to eat only when I'm hungry and stop eating when I'm satisfied. I've learned to eat foods closest to their natural state.

After gaining this wisdom, I struggled to increase my self-control. I asked God for the strength to overcome temptations. He whispered, "Put Me first." I was, and still am, to a lesser degree, tempted by sweets and junk food. Sometimes I still want to eat for fun or comfort or from boredom instead of merely hunger. But self-control is improving. When I remember to put God first in my thoughts, food temptations fade into the background.

Going to the Lord daily, sometimes hourly, asking for help to work through my problem, has increased my faith. He assures me I can trust Him. This gives me the courage to persevere toward my goal.

God's loving compassion, forgiving me when I fail and strengthening me when I'm weak, has given me compassion for others struggling with the same problem. I've learned to be patient with myself and others. I've learned to wait and listen for God's guidance. My eating behavior at times is still unlovely, but I no longer believe *I* am unlovable.

## *Prayer*

***Dear God, thank You for walking with me through each day's lessons.***

## Affirmation

I'm taking the steps from faith to love.

# A PARTY

***Be strong in the Lord and in his mighty power (Ephesians 6:10).***

It was a situation loaded with triggers for an eating binge. My husband and I had invited twenty people over for dinner. We wanted to welcome our nephew and his new bride to our community.

Before I opened the cookbook and started my grocery list, I prayed for strength. *Lord, I need to spend a lot of time thinking about food for this party. Don't let it trigger me into an eating binge.* The Lord reminded me of Ephesians 6:10.

As I began working on the menu, my mind filled with thoughts of the sweet newlyweds. I forgot about bingeing.

The day before the party, I filled the house with the aroma of baking bread and cakes. The smell teased the trigger for bingeing. *Lord, I need a little extra help. Part of me wants to sit down with a tub of butter and a loaf of warm bread and eat it all!*

My prayer was shortened by the sound of an upset cow. She stood across our fenced yard mooing for her calf, which was tramping across my herb garden! I dashed out the door, chasing the calf around the garden and across the yard. With one youthful jump, he cleared the cattle guard and raced toward his mother. By the time I repaired the damage, the aroma of freshly baked bread had faded from my kitchen.

The day of the party, I set aside thirty minutes to be alone with God before I started my cooking. *Lord, grant me Your peace as I prepare this food. Please keep me from nervously eating all day long.*

Relaxed and confident in God's peace, I cooked the entire day and ate only my usual breakfast and a light lunch. I vanquished the urges to nibble with quick prayers for God's "mighty power."

After the last guest said goodbye, I plopped into a chair and propped up my feet. I thought with surprise, *Lord, You got me through it; I didn't binge!*

***Lord, thank You for victory over banquets and binges.***

## Affirmation

God helps me through one dinner party at a time.

# *PRAISEWORTHY THOUGHTS*

***Finally, brothers, whatever is true, whatever is noble, whatever is right, whatever is pure, whatever is lovely, whatever is admirable—if anything is excellent or praiseworthy—think about such things (Philippians 4:8).***

We moved from St. Louis, a metropolitan area of 2.5 million, to our ranch in Idaho. The nearest town—population fifty-two—is ten miles away. Nearly a mile away, hidden in a grove of blue spruces, is our nearest neighbor's home.

In a letter to our relatives in Indiana, I described our paradise: "When I inhale the clear, clean air, I want to gulp it down into my thirsty lungs. As I walk the half-mile lane to our mailbox, I'm surrounded by open ranges and majestic mountains. The tangy scent of sagebrush wafts through the air. The call of Canada geese or the quiet warbling of a mountain bluebird is a daily musical performance. Absent are the roaring traffic, loud music, and sirens. No place on earth can equal this splendor."

A relative arrived for a visit and came to a different point of view. "It's so desolate! The silence is eerie. How do you stand it here?"

The sights, sounds, smells, and textures that created within me an attitude of awe failed to impress my guest. As Milton said in *Paradise Lost*, "The mind is its own place, and in itself / Can make a Heav'n of Hell, a Hell of Heav'n."

I can see the disciplined life of proper nutrition and exercise as either deprivation or "growth in grace and character" (Hebrews 12:11, TLB). I can envision myself zipping through the workday with a song and a skip or dragging through each daily task with sighs and dread.

What is true? God will help me overcome a food addiction.

What is pure? Fresh fruits and vegetables.

What is lovely? A new dress in a smaller size.

What is admirable? Staying with my plan.

What is excellent? Better health.

What is praiseworthy? Encouraging other overweights.

***Heavenly Father, help me think praiseworthy thoughts.***

## Affirmation

My thoughts are on excellent things.

# *RED SHOES*

***You came near when I called you, and you said, "Do not fear" (Lamentations 3:57).***

One morning as I raced around my bedroom getting dressed for a shopping trip, my teenage daughter barged into my room, still wearing her housecoat.

"Mom, can I look in your closet? I don't have anything to wear."

"I thought you said my clothes were 'frumpy.' "

"Oh, that was yesterday. They might look better today."

I laughed and told her to go ahead. Two minutes later she called to me from inside my walk-in closet.

"Do you know that every pair of shoes you own is a shade of brown?"

"No, they aren't!"

"Come look for yourself."

I joined her in my closet and was surprised to see she was right! My shoes ranged from beige to dark brown, with various heights of heels.

"Mom, what are you trying to hide with your frumpy

clothes and brown shoes?"

"Nothing," I laughed weakly. "Go put on your blue blouse and jeans. It's time to go."

The next day, when the house was quiet, I went back into my closet to examine my shoes with a new perspective. There lay all my brown shoes, lined up as witnesses to my low self-esteem. Next, I surveyed my clothes. My daughter was right; they were "frumpy"! What *was* I trying to hide?

*Me. I'm trying to hide myself!* Just as I use my weight to hide behind, I'm using my shoes and clothes as well. I'm afraid that if someone notices me, I might not measure up. I might get hurt; even worse, things might get beyond my control. I'm trying to hide my fears.

I never realized how much fear I carry around with me each day. Today I'm going to bundle up my fears and hand them to God. I'll throw in the fear of getting my feelings hurt, the fear of losing control of my emotions, and the fear of losing the approval of my family and friends.

I need to be aware of when these fears start influencing my behavior. A good warning signal to watch for is overeating. Each time I catch myself wanting to binge, I know it's time to see why I'm trying to hide. Identifying fears and turning them over to God leads to victory.

The color of victory surely isn't brown. I think I'll go buy a pair of *red* shoes!

## *Prayer*

***Thank You, Lord, for taking my bundle of fears.***

## Affirmation

"The Lord is my light and my salvation—whom shall I fear?" (Psalm 27:1).

# *PEACH TREE*

***I am the Lord, the God of all mankind. Is anything too hard for me? (Jeremiah 32:27).***

Lovers of fresh fruit, my husband and I planted two peach trees in our backyard. Although we knew it would take three to five years before the trees would produce a crop, we were willing to wait for our very own orchard.

The trees were barely in the ground one month when a dump truck buried one sapling in gravel. We shoveled the rocks aside, fearing that our little peach tree was hopelessly damaged. We discovered a few tiny green leaves still clinging to the branches. Taking heart, we watered it throughout the next two summers, hoping for the best.

The third season after planting our trees, they yielded a crop. The tree once buried in gravel produced such an abundance of peaches that its branches bent to the ground from the weight. The unharmed fruit tree bore three peaches.

My husband thought possibly the lime from the gravel fertilized the young tree, giving us the bumper crop. I like to think that it was the little tree's way of thanking us for digging it out and treating it with hope.

Sometimes I feel like that sapling buried in rocks. The worries and frustrations of living in an overpopulated world crush me with feelings of helplessness. I catch myself overeating to calm psychological stress, comfort jittery nerves, or escape endless demands. Yet I know God is there, willing to dig me out and offer me hope. I must remember to thank Him by bearing good fruit with my life.

## Prayer

***Heavenly Father, help me remember that nothing is too hard for You even in this overcrowded, complex world.***

## Affirmation

I am thankful for God's care.

# BOX OF FEARS

***Fear of man will prove to be a snare, but whoever trusts in the Lord is kept safe (Proverbs 29:25).***

The UPS man delivered the plant I'd ordered from a nursery in another state. Eagerly, I cut the tape on the box and flipped up the lid. Glancing into the box, I saw something scurry under the packing paper. As the echo of my scream bounced off the ceiling, I heard tiny feet scratching inside the cardboard. Adrenalin surged through my body as visions of mice and rats grew in my imagination. Shivering with fear, I dropped a large book on the lid and waited for my husband, Judd, to come home.

When Judd arrived, I immediately told him about the box full of rats the UPS man had delivered. Realizing that my creative mind was probably working overtime again but seeing that my fear was real, he carried the box outside to open it. Judd found my plant—and a tiny lizard.

Growing a giant fear from the footsteps of a tiny creature is an example of my frequent reaction to life. I accumulate endless little worries and allow them to magnify in my mind. Fear becomes a habit that no longer reflect reality. I go through the day opening boxes of anxiety, then slamming the lid shut. Unable to confront my concerns, I imagine them as monsters of terror. Worrying and fretting lead to a nervous eating binge as I attempt to soothe my fears.

Today, each time I felt anxiety growing, I handed God my box of fears. He gave me back cartons of calm, confidence, and courage. As my false fears shrank, so did my false appetite.

## *Prayer*

***Today, Lord, I felt victorious each time I released a fear to You. Help my trust in You to grow.***

## Affirmation

"The only power which can resist the power of fear is the power of love" (Alan Paton).

# WE'RE MAGNIFICENT

***How great is the love the Father has lavished on us, that we should be called children of God! And that is what we are! The reason the world does not know us is that it did not know him (1 John 3:1).***

"Each of you is ordinary and magnificent," the speaker at our women's retreat said. "You go to the grocery store, buy brown bread and yellow cheese, and hope you can pay for it. The small details of your lives are important."

I never thought of myself as "magnificent." When CNN shows an illiterate, starving African woman walking miles and miles to find help for her baby, I believe that woman is magnificent. Tornado victims who have lost all they owned and yet say, "We still have our family; that's all that's important"—those people are magnificent.

I hear the expression "Get the big picture." Maybe the big picture is that I am as magnificent as that African woman or the tornado victims simply because I'm a child of God.

Maybe it is the little, everyday things we do that make

us marvelous. Perhaps the big things are the frills.

God *does* care about the small details in my life. He wants to give me victory over my food addiction. When I focus on the small details of everyday living, I am allowing His mastery over my compulsive eating. I start my day praying for guidance with my food choices for that day. Then I jot down my meal plans and ask God to give me the strength to stick to them. He gives me the victory.

How many centuries have men and women planned and prepared meals for their families? How many times have men and women thanked God for the food they were about to eat? How many men and women have praised God for the small victories in their everyday lives?

## *Prayer*

***Heavenly Father, thank You for giving me victory over the small details in my life.***

## Affirmation

My magnificent God made me magnificent too.

# *REWARDS*

***I the Lord search the heart and examine the mind, to reward a man according to his conduct, according to what his deeds deserve (Jeremiah 17:10).***

After the excitement of the first snowstorm, Christmas, and the Valentine's Day party, my second-grade class became despondent. Spring seemed far away, and their schoolwork became drudgery. One day I arrived at school carrying something round and long over my shoulder.

Eight-year-olds love to guess about surprises. The room filled with chattering as I whisked the strange object to the corner of the classroom near the bookcases. With a snap of my wrists, I unrolled the mystery.

"O-o-oh!" my students said in unison. Each reached down to rub the fake-fur rug. "It's so soft! May we sit on it?"

"Yes."

Twenty-five boys and girls simultaneously attempted to sit on the 7' x 9' rug. Before a war started, I said, "I think we need a plan for sharing."

After a short discussion, we decided on a point system. When they had earned twenty-five points, they could select a book, plunk down on the fuzzy rug, and snuggle in its softness for fifteen uninterrupted minutes. They suggested various ways to earn points: finishing their assignments, helping a classmate, picking up trash.

Receiving a reward of free time on the fuzzy rug remained a thrill until the first sunny spring day. It helped us through the boring winter plateau.

Everyone who has endeavored to lose weight understands plateau despondency. We need "rewards" merely to keep striving. God gives us many rewards besides food. How about trying one of these: (1) Treat yourself to a new book—plus the time to read it. (2) Buy something new to wear, even if you will need to alter it to a smaller size later. (3) Make a phone call to a faraway friend. (4) Buy a puppy or kitten—adults enjoy soft, fuzzy rewards too.

***Lord, help me remember that eating proper foods and exercising daily will eventually result in slimness, energy, and health.***

## Affirmation

God will reward my efforts.

# *SUNSET*

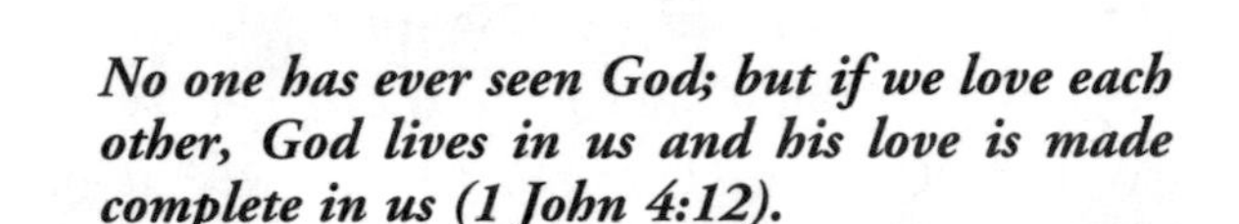

***No one has ever seen God; but if we love each other, God lives in us and his love is made complete in us (1 John 4:12).***

Springs are hectic on an Idaho ranch. Calves kick and run in every direction, testing every inch of the fence. Fields have grown a whole new crop of rocks that need to be picked up and carried away. Irrigation pipes need repair and placement.

One particular spring, my husband and I raced our separate ways through several days of labor. The strain on our bodies and spirits began to show. As always, we drew to each other for comfort.

Hand in hand, we walked to the back pasture, inhaling the soft spring air. Leaning against the log fence, we silently watched the sky change from bright pink to deep purple as the sun eased down behind a mountain peak. Nature's soothing show melted our stress. As we strolled back toward the house feeling rejuvenated, my husband slipped his arm around my waist and said, "Your love gives meaning to beautiful sunsets."

His tender words sustained me through the long days

of work that followed. Then one cold November evening we snuggled together on the couch before a warm fire. I asked him if he remembered that spring sunset. He gave me a squeeze and answered, "It goes double for sunrises."

The beauty, tenderness, and strength shared in the love between a husband and wife is only a hint at the depth of God's love for us.

I can feel physically miserable from making wrong food choices. I can hate my behavior as an overeater. But I should never feel unlovable. God knows more about my weaknesses than I do, yet He loves me. He gives me sunsets to help me relax and evaluate my decisions. He gives me sunrises to start new days in which I can grow toward being all He knows I can be.

## *Prayer*

***Heavenly Father, thank You for your faith in me.***

## Affirmation

I'm a beloved child of God.



4—T.B.M.

# SEEDLINGS OF PRAYER

***If one falls down, his friend can help him up. But pity the man who falls and has no one to help him up (Ecclesiastes 4:10).***

One late winter afternoon, Harriet and I worked in her greenhouse, transplanting herb seedlings into larger containers. Feeling like a new mother, I burst out enthusiastically, "Oh, I want every tiny seedling to live and grow!"

Harriet glanced up at me and answered in total seriousness, "I pray over my plants, don't you?"

"I guess I never thought about it, but I'm sure it would be all right. After all, God made us stewards of the earth."

"Let's pray right now," Harriet replied.

I felt a little strange at first, praying for such things as mint, chamomile, and thyme, but it made me feel close to God and His creation.

After our prayer, we silently continued digging in the potting soil. I began to think about Harriet's faith. She radiates an absolute confidence in God's interest in every area of her life and prays about *everything.* A new thought entered my mind. If she believes God attends to something as small as my herb seeds, she might also believe He would be concerned about my compulsive overeating. Perhaps she will even pray with me about it. Although she doesn't have a weight problem, she has compassion. Most important of all, she has a strong faith that God can handle anything we bring to Him.

With great trepidation, I decided to risk asking her to pray with me about something as personal as my struggle with food abuse. "Harriet, will you pray with me for my freedom from compulsive overeating?" I held my breath, waiting for the sting of a laugh or a lecture on what I "should" do.

She stopped digging in the seed beds and looked directly at me. "I'd be honored to."

A rush of relief flooded my body as I released my breath. We joined our muddy hands in prayer at that moment. Harriet prayed: "Lord, I thank You for this opportunity to share with Pauline a reminder of Your absolute sovereignty in our lives. I join with her in praying that she can release this problem to You."

Tears of assurance filled my eyes as the strength of victory filled my heart. I wished I'd had the courage to ask a friend to pray with me sooner. I experienced more victory at that point than I'd ever had in my prayers alone.

## Prayer

***Thank You, heavenly Father, for caring Christian friends.***

## Affirmation

"Our job is not to straighten each other out, but help each other up" (Neva Coyle).

# *KEYS*

***If you call out for insight and cry aloud for understanding, and if you look for it as for silver and search for it as for hidden treasure, then you will understand the fear of the Lord and find the knowledge of God (Proverbs 2:3-5).***

My seven-year-old son sauntered into the kitchen, carrying a shovel and a box full of old keys.

"What are you planning to do with that shovel?" I asked.

"Going to bury a bunch of keys in the backyard."

He was proud of his old-key collection. I knew he saw it as burying his "treasure." "OK, but be sure to dig only in the back where we don't have any grass or flowers."

"I know, Mom."

"Don't forget to mark where you bury the keys if you want to find them again."

He nodded his head and strolled on outside.

I had completely forgotten about his buried treasure until I arrived home from work one day and found him once again digging in our backyard. This time he had dug more than a dozen holes! He was in a panic, for the marker had disappeared, and he couldn't find his cache of keys. Off and on all summer, he went from spot to spot, digging holes, searching for his treasures. He never found them.

When I search from diet to diet, trying to find the key to weight control, I have no more luck than my son had in finding his keys. I dig into the diet books with hope and determination, only to fail at finding permanent weight loss.

Today, I walked away from all those holes in diet theories and simply asked God where the markers are supposed to be. He told me to look under the rock marked "willingness." There I found two shovels marked "abstinence" and "healing." I asked a friend to help me dig for my keys to victory over food abuse. We prayed together, then began digging. We found the box of keys; it was labeled "Overeaters Anonymous' Twelve Steps to Recovery."

## Prayer

***Lord, I praise You and thank You for guidance and group support on my road to victorious recovery.***

## Affirmation

My Higher Power is the Christian God.

# CHILDISH GAMES

***When I was a child, I talked like a child, I thought like a child, I reasoned like a child. When I became a man, I put childish ways behind me (1 Corinthians 13:11).***

When I was a child growing up on a farm in Indiana, I had a favorite hideaway. I slipped behind the gray barn, darted between hickory and sweet maple trees, then scurried down a steep hill to my secret spot.

A shallow creek bubbled and chuckled through the tiny valley, but in a few spots it formed pools deep enough for swimming. In the summer, I'd grab a grapevine, swing out over the pool, and let go for the plunge. Sometimes I was a cannonball shot at an enemy ship; other times I was Mighty Mouse, flying to save a drowning person.

When the days were too cool for swimming, I sat on a large limb that protruded over the water. I was Sacagawea in a canoe with Lewis and Clark or a Pilgrim on the *Mayflower* headed for Plymouth Rock, worrying about what lurked in the dense forest ahead.

My imaginary games were limitless. They became so engrossing that my mother often startled me when she called me to lunch.

Today, I still play games in which I distort reality. For example, I tell myself:

1. I'm buying these cookies just for the kids. (But they're my favorite brand.)

2. Being a good wife and mother means baking homemade sweets for my family. (What about *their* proper nutrition?)

3. I've already blown my diet. I'll start again on Monday. (How many Monday-diet-days paraded past!)

4. I can't diet now; I'm too tired or under too much stress. ("Come to me, all you who are weary and burdened, and I will give you rest."—Matthew 11:28.)

## Prayer

***Lord Jesus, help me put away my childish games. Help me use my rich imagination to visualize the real benefits of a healthier, thinner body.***

## Affirmation

"I put childish ways behind me."

# *HERE'S THE DEAL*

***There is a proper time and procedure for every matter (Ecclesiastes 8:6).***

I sighed with relief as I stepped out of my slippers and pulled the bedspread back on my bed. *What an exhausting day. How did it get to be midnight so soon?* I slid under the covers and reached for the lamp. Before I could turn off the light, my teenage daughter bounced into my bedroom.

"Mom, here's the deal!"

I cringed inside, knowing I didn't really want to hear about "the deal."

"You know those cream-cheese brownies you make?" She took a deep breath and continued, "The ones that are so chewy and delicious and that everyone thinks are the very best in the whole world. Well, I told the kids in our drama club you wouldn't mind baking some for our fund-raiser. You will, won't you, Mom?"

"Well, I guess I can. When do you need them?"

"Tomorrow."

"Tomorrow! By what time?"

"Oh, not 'til 8:00 or 8:30."

"In the morning? You can forget it! I need time to buy

the ingredients, bake them—and I suppose you'll want them delivered too."

"I'm sorry, Mom, I just forgot to tell you sooner. You can do it. I'll run to the store for you now. Then you can bake them before I go to school in the morning. Brownies don't take long, do they?"

"If you'd take the time to learn to cook, you'd know how long brownies take!"

At 6:00 a.m., we *both* rolled out of bed to bake brownies together. That was *my* "deal." I helped my daughter, but according to my rules.

Sometimes I think I try starting my mornings off with this prayer: "God, 'here's the deal.' I want to be free of my overeating compulsion by 8:00 or 8:30 a.m." Of course, God doesn't work that way. He helps me, but I must follow His rules. He prepares me for the changes I need to make according to His timetable.

***Lord, I leave the timing and procedure to You for my victory over compulsive eating.***

## Affirmation

There's a great "deal" of victory with God's timetable.

# *INVISIBLE WALLS*

***It was faith that brought the walls of Jericho tumbling down (Hebrews 11:30, TLB).***

The tapping sound drew me into the living room. I stood silently, straining to locate the sound. Then a flutter at the window caught my eye. A tiny hummingbird was charging the windowpane, trying to reach my giant red geranium.

The determined bird maintained his attacks off and on throughout the morning. Finally, I decided to move the geranium before he seriously injured himself. After I moved the plant, the hummingbird flew back and forth, up and down, searching for his red treasure. He simply couldn't understand the invisible wall that had separated him from his goal.

What is the invisible wall that separates me from victory over my battle with weight? Am I blindly battering against old beliefs and habits? I can't ask God to remove my temptation because I can't completely give up eating. I can ask God, instead, to do a bigger job for me—to make my invisible wall come tumbling down.

Each day, through one learning experience at a time, I can see cracks forming in my barrier to proper eating. Old habits and beliefs about what tastes good are being changed by God's Holy Spirit working in me. For example, I learned that I get the same vitamins and minerals from skim milk as I do from whole milk. I've developed a taste for skim milk and now find whole milk too rich.

Through God's power, the wall that separates me from a slender, healthy body is beginning to crumble.

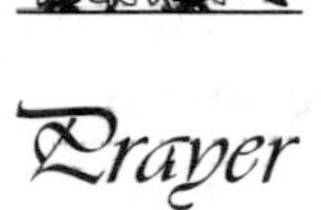


***Thank You, Lord, for breaking down my invisible walls with one victorious tap at a time.***

## Affirmation

Through faith and obedience, my walls come tumbling down.

# OBESITY

***Be joyful in hope, patient in affliction, faithful in prayer (Romans 12:12).***

Many doctors consider obesity an incurable disease. Some say it's genetic. My father weighed over two hundred fifty pounds, and my grandmother inched close to three hundred. How can I fight my genes? That sounds like an even better excuse than saying I'm "big-boned." For some reason I ignore the fact that my mother weighed barely one hundred pounds and my grandfather was tall and slender.

Most doctors also say obesity is controllable. Whether a genetic or an emotional affliction, obesity can be controlled through weight loss and a lifelong eating plan.

Psychologists tell us most overweights are great self-deceivers. We lack a sense of reality. When we overeat, we don't accept the consequences of our actions. We pretend that if we eat standing up, or, better yet, hide in the pantry, the calories won't count.

But the most common and difficult trait for overweights to deal with is impatience. In the past I've dieted for a few days, even for a week, then weighed. If I weighed the same, I became impatient. If I'd lost weight, it wasn't enough. Impatience led to despair, then on to a binge. I deceived myself into thinking a "cookie will make it better" when, in fact, it led only to deeper despair.

The Lord gave me common sense. When I listen to it, I know I can't change a lifelong way of living in one week. I will pray for a clearer sense of reality. I will develop patience by following a sensible eating plan for life. Developing patience and realism isn't easy; the Lord never promised ease. It is possible, however, especially when I lean on the Lord in prayer.

The joy comes with a sense of purpose, a goal to work toward, a feeling of accomplishment as the weeks slip by and the pounds slip away.

## Prayer

*Father, thank You for opening my eyes to self-deceptions.*

## Affirmation

The Lord gives me the joy of hope and patience to overcome.

# PACING

***Do you not know that in a race all the runners run, but only one gets the prize? Run in such a way as to get the prize (1 Corinthians 9:24).***

When my youngest child entered kindergarten, I returned to college to finish my degree in education. Although I was several years older than most of my classmates, it never presented a problem until I took the class Methods for Teaching Physical Education. This class required the students to pass a physical-fitness test that they would someday give to their students.

The balance beam gave me no problems—hand-and-eye-coordination skills were a snap. Gymnastics proved a little difficult, yet passable. But the endurance I needed to run a mile remained beyond my ability. Each class period, I tried and failed. Time was running out. I prayed for strength, for an alternate activity—anything to help me pass this necessary task.

With only three days left until the class ended, I once again started to jog around the track in still another attempt to pass the test. Then a young boy in my class jogged easily up beside me. "All you need," he said, with a bright, energetic smile, "is pacing. Run along with me, keeping my pace." With a relaxed flow of steps, he made it seem easy. Changing my running pattern, locking into his rhythm, and concentrating on his constant encouraging comments transformed my mind; my body obeyed. Soon I completed the mile—and the class.

As I race through the day's activities, I see the Lord running beside me, monitoring my pace. He sets my mind and heart to the rhythm that He originally planned for my body to make it healthy and energetic.

## Prayer

***Father, help me lock step with You. By exercising my body, I know I can gain the prize of health and energy. By exercising my mind and spirit, I will win the crown that lasts forever.***

## Affirmation

I am keeping pace with God's plan for me.

# WEEDS

***Get rid of all bitterness, rage and anger, brawling and slander, along with every form of malice (Ephesians 4:31).***

While muttering to myself, I hacked at the weeds in my herb garden. *He makes me so mad!* I yanked out weeds and slung them into the wheelbarrow. *It isn't fair.* I heaved the heavy load over to the compost pile and flung it onto the top of the heap. *He's trying to take advantage of my good nature.*

For the next hour, I chopped, shoveled, yanked, hurled, and muttered. As I worked, my pace began to slow. The hoe once again became a tool instead of an instrument of vengeance. The weeds became my true object of attention, instead of my anger. My muttering mellowed.

*Maybe I exaggerated a little bit.* I tugged at a weed, being careful not to break it off without getting the root. *He did have one valid point.* I wheeled the small load of weeds to the compost pile, stopping to gaze up at the mountains before dumping the debris. *Perhaps if I told him I recognized his position, he would be willing to listen to mine.*

When the fight had erupted, I'd stormed out of the house and stood on the deck crying in anger. "Lord, I am so-o-o angry. Help me!"

God said, "Go pull weeds."

Heading for the toolshed, I'd muttered, "Great. I ask God to help, and He gives me more work to do. Some big help He is." Yet, I obeyed. Usually, I deny my anger, call it hurt feelings, and wallow in self-pity and chocolate.

As I walked back to my garden with the empty wheelbarrow, I felt emptied of my burden of rage. Each step I took back toward my garden, I felt closer to freedom from food addiction. For the first time in my life, I wasn't trying to stuff down my anger with food. I wasn't denying it, hiding it, or suppressing it. I had dealt with it in an appropriate manner. Without realizing it, I'd released it.

With God's guidance, I'd triumphed over my longtime habit of dealing with anger by going on an eating binge. I burst out in praise, "Lord, You used weeds to make me a winner!"

## *Prayer*

***Lord of victory, thank You for showing me how to deal with my anger without turning to food abuse.***

## Affirmation

With God's help, I'm a winner.

# *JOE JUMP BASIN*

***Every valley shall be filled in, every mountain and hill made low (Luke 3:5).***

One sunny morning in late spring, my husband rushed into the house. "Pack a lunch and grab a coat. I want you to go with us to Joe Jump Basin. The view up there is unbelievable!"

The ranch foreman, my husband, and I loaded our four-wheel bikes with food, water, shovels, and various other tools. The main objective of the trip was to repair a watering trough.

We started the climb up the mountain in single file. Each minute that we scaled upward, the terrain became rougher and steeper. At times I felt as if my bike defied gravity with its sharp upward tilt. I glanced behind me for a second to see whether my husband was still following. Seeing how far I'd climbed made me lightheaded.

I had no choice but to keep climbing. Finally, we made it to the top, where the terrain leveled out. My husband was right; the view was phenomenal.

This was a special moment to share with my husband, a time to draw close and share the spectacle of God's workmanship. My husband slipped his big hand over mine and said, "I couldn't wait for you to see this."

I missed the moment's romance. In near hysteria, I screeched, "How will I ever get down from here?"

My husband calmly answered, "Just take it slowly."

The rest of the morning I worried about the trip back. The picnic lunch stuck in my throat. My mouth remained parched, regardless of how much water I drank.

After the men had repaired the trough, we began the trip home. When we came to the summit, I put my four-wheeler in super-low gear and crept down the mountain. The men waited patiently at the bottom. To my surprise, it was less frightening than the climb upward. When I arrived where the men were waiting, our ranch foreman said, "You're amazing. I'd never get my wife to attempt a steep climb like that."

A sensation of extreme bravery flooded over me. (I never mentioned my terror.)

Deciding to overcome my food addiction filled me with similar fear. How could I possibly do it? The Lord said, "Take it slowly."

Each day I creep toward my goal. The progress feels good. The sensations of bravery and accomplishment spur me onward.

## *Prayer*

***Thank You, Lord, for lowering my mountain.***

## Affirmation

I can do it.

# *INCREASE MY FAITH*

***"Lord, if it's you," Peter replied, "tell me to come to you on the water." "Come," he said. Then Peter got down out of the boat and walked on the water to Jesus (Matthew 14:28, 29).***

No one wanted the sixth-grade class in Vacation Bible School. Our planning committee grumbled about their impertinent attitude. But I'd finished a year with second graders and decided it would be a welcome change to work with older children.

With enthusiasm, I created detailed lesson plans, combining visual aids and thought-provoking discussion questions. Every day I prayed for the students coming to my class. I desired an open, attentive heart and petitioned Christ to speak through me. Like Peter's, my faith was strong. I stepped out of the boat and into the sixth-grade classroom.

The second morning, Jason sneered at Mona, "You're too stupid to memorize Bible verses." Mona cried. Her best friend fired back a defense. "Jason, you're too ugly for anyone to listen to, even if you can memorize." This aroused the loyalty of Jason's best friend. I felt myself sinking into the tide.

The third morning, the battle lines were drawn between the sexes. I sank to my waist.

On the fourth morning, the girls glared silently at the boys. The boys ignored the girls while muttering negative comments among themselves. Fear overwhelmed my weakened faith. Imitating Peter, I called out to Christ and received His help. We put aside the fancy lesson plans and held a circle prayer and sharing session. The class time ended with love (even hugs) flowing from each young heart.

I often begin a diet with immense faith and enthusiasm. Then when temptations weaken me, I lose my confidence that God cares enough to help me. I begin to sink. Like Peter, I need to cry out, "Lord, save me!" When Peter asked for help, "Immediately Jesus reached out his hand and caught him" (verse 31). That same hand will also lift me.

***Lord Jesus, forgive my doubts. Increase my faith.***

## Affirmation

My faith is strong. I can feel trust welling up within me.

# PASS ON THE GIVING

***Give, and it will be given to you. A good measure, pressed down, shaken together and running over, will be poured into your lap. For with the measure you use, it will be measured to you (Luke 6:38).***

When I started walking every day as part of my exercise program, my husband gave me a small cassette player with headphones. His actions said, "I support your efforts. I'm on your side. I'm willing to invest in your success. I have faith in you."

My son followed his father's lead in putting his support into action. He presented me with a cassette tape of praise songs. The peppy music motivates me to walk briskly.

Each day I lace up my sneakers, pop the tape into my cassette player, and head down our lane to the beat of stereo music. The lively music sends energy surging through my body, adding a spring to each step. Singing along with praises to God lifts my spirits in joyful worship. Since the cassette player and tape are gifts of love, I feel surrounded by the warmth and caring of my family.

I can do one other thing to make my gifts complete—

I can pass on the giving. Today I can give others the support and encouragement they need to meet their challenges. I can share humor and laughter. I can listen. I can give a helping hand in an unpleasant task. I can say, "I love your perfume!" Maybe they'll hear, "You have excellent taste; you're an excellent person." I can give comforting words, time, or material gifts. I don't need to return a gift to a giver but can instead pass on the giving. No matter how wealthy, we are all in need of encouragement.

## Prayer

***Father, thank You for the joy of giving as well as receiving.***

## Affirmation

I can never outgive God.

# GREAT DELIGHT

***The Lord your God is with you, he is mighty to save. He will take great delight in you, he will quiet you with his love, he will rejoice over you with singing (Zephaniah 3:17).***

I loved him—even before the doctor placed the tiny infant on my abdomen and said, "You have a son!" I knew nothing about this child, not even the color of his eyes, but my intense love for him flowed over in tears of joy.

I wanted to wrap him in my arms to quiet his cries. I wanted to sing him lullabies and share with him what great delight he gave me. I would care for him and protect him with my very life.

When my baby took his first breath, something clicked in my mind. Could God love *me* this much?

As far back as I could remember, I had a low self-concept. From the moment of my son's birth, however, I began to understand God's love. His love just is—no strings attached.

Now my son is grown and away at college. When he calls, I ask him, "Are you eating right? Do you get enough rest? Don't sit at your desk all the time; get some exercise too." I worry about him taking proper care of himself.

He makes me happy when he replies, "Mom, I eat a salad every day, and I ride my bike to school. I'm doing fine."

As God's beloved child, I realize I'm pleasing Him when I take care of myself also. Moderate eating, rest, and exercise are the habits of people who know they are loved.

## Prayer

***Thank You, heavenly Father, for loving me.***

## Affirmation

Today I will take good care of God's beloved child, me.

# TIMING

***Let us then fearlessly and confidently and boldly draw near to the throne of grace—the throne of God's unmerited favor [to us sinners]; that we may receive mercy [for our failures] and find grace to help in good time for every need—appropriate help and well-timed help, coming just when we need it (Hebrews 4:16, Amplified).***

During my daughter's college years, she shared a house with three girlfriends. Only one of the girls, Jean, could cook. My daughter explained it this way: "Jean is a great cook, but she still needs to work on her timing."

"What do you mean?" I asked.

"You know, Mom, when *you* cook a meal, everything is ready at the same time. With Jean, the rolls might get done and maybe the potatoes. We eat those. After a while she finishes the dessert and the salad. So we eat those. It might be an hour or two later when we eat the entree. I don't know how you get the timing so perfect."

My timing with meals may be perfect, but it had been less than perfect when it came to weight loss. I'd get out the calendar and think: *Now if I lose three pounds a week, I'll be able to get into my favorite dress for the big event in six weeks.* Yet, my plans and my timing never came out right. I rarely stuck with my strategy for more than a week or two. This invariably led to disappointment, self-disgust, then a food binge.

Now, however, I begin my day by turning my eating and activity schedule over to God. I relax and willingly release to Him my lack of self-control. I ask for help in abstaining from sweets and refined carbohydrates and in planning balanced meals. I also ask God for the motivation to exercise. All the parts of the process come together perfectly when I put God in charge of the timing.

One day at a time, I "fearlessly and confidently and boldly draw near to the throne of grace," asking God to do for me what I cannot do myself. I discover His "well-timed help, coming just when [I] need it."

## Prayer

***Thank You, Jesus, for the victory of Your perfect timing in my life.***

## Affirmation

I take time to ask for God's timing.

# RETROSPECTION

***I can do everything through him who gives me strength (Philippians 4:13).***

I glared at the bathroom mirror, daring my eyes to discover one more gray hair. My husband strolled in with a smile and said cheerfully, "There's my birthday girl!"

Feeling unbearably old, I trudged into our bedroom, slumped down on our bed, and began to bawl.

My husband slipped down beside me, circling my shoulder with his arm, trying to comfort me. "Honey, it's not so bad turning forty. Think how you've grown spiritually and emotionally in forty years, making your life richer and happier."

I absorbed as much sympathy as he had time to give, then promised I'd try keeping a positive attitude the rest of the day.

After he left for work, I contemplated my forty years. What living patterns had I developed that made my life "richer and happier"?

1. I've stopped believing my self-worth is based on the approval of others. I'm a child of God; that makes me

valuable. I do my best; He forgives my weaknesses.

2. I've developed the courage to take risks. I went back to finish my college degree at twenty-nine. I learned to ride a horse at thirty-five. I tried learning to ski at thirty-nine. Overcoming the fears associated with each activity opened joyful worlds I never suspected existed.

3. I stopped blaming situations and other people for my problems. I ask myself, "This is the situation; what am *I* going to do about it?"

My husband was right. I had cultivated enriching behavior patterns. Why not extend these lessons to my weight problem? For example: (1) Being overweight doesn't make me a worthless person. I'm a beloved child of God, regardless of size. (2) I possess the courage to risk the changes that occur when I lose weight. (3) Regardless of what or who made me fat, I'm the only one to do something about it.

***Lord, thank You for helping me develop my potential.***

## Affirmation

I'm working on my weight problem *today.*

# *RICHARD'S CAKE*

***If I have walked in falsehood or my foot has hurried after deceit—let God weigh me in honest scales and he will know that I am blameless (Job 31:5, 6).***

Richard, our foreman's teenage son, spent a day at our house washing windows. As he worked, I did my weekend baking.

"Is that chocolate cake I smell?" he asked. "I sure like chocolate cake. Dad and I aren't much good at baking cakes."

"I tell you what," I answered. "I promised this one for a bake sale, but I'll bake you and your dad one next week."

"Great!"

The following Tuesday I gave Richard's dad, Jay, a chocolate cake to take home. At lunchtime, Jay decided to share the cake with a bachelor co-worker who seldom got home-baked goodies. The men enjoyed it so much that they decided not to share it with Richard. "What he doesn't know won't hurt him," they conspired. They didn't realize I'd promised the cake to Richard. The two cowboys hid the cake in the bunkhouse and ate it all in two days.

Later in the week, I saw Richard and asked him how he liked the cake.

"I thought you forgot!" he answered. He quickly found his dad to get the true story.

When I heard what had happened, I baked Richard another cake. As I personally handed Richard the cake, I winked at Jay and stifled a grin while saying, "Here's the cake I promised you. You can decide who you want to share it with."

With a broad smile Richard answered, "Dad's not getting any, even if he has tears in his eyes while he watches me eat it."

The teasing was in fun, but I understood an underlying truth. Sometimes I tease myself, saying, "No one will know I ate a second (or third) piece of cake." Of course, I get caught when my jeans become too tight to zip. Then it's not funny.

When I overeat, it's not God's guidance I'm listening to. It's my own. Today I'll be honest with myself about what I eat.

## *Prayer*

***Help me to pray like Job, with a clear conscience.***

## Affirmation

I don't kid myself about what I eat.

# TAKE MY PAIN

***Praise be to the Lord, for he has heard my cry for mercy (Psalm 28:6).***

One day while Wendy and I were riding our horses, we heard the howling of an animal in pain. Once we located the direction of the sound, we kicked our horses into a canter and raced toward it.

As we neared the animal, Wendy stopped me. "It's a dog; I can see him. He's caught in a trap. If he's in as much pain as it sounds, we'll have to be careful. All he understands is his pain. He'll strike out at anything that comes near him."

Wendy was right. After we dismounted and walked closer, the little dog tried to attack us.

Each step we came closer to the hurting animal, the more vicious he became. His tormented cries tearing at our hearts, we stared from a safe distance, not knowing how to help. Then, as if he could bear no more, the dog stopped snarling and lay down. He seemed barely conscious.

"Quick," Wendy said, "grab your horse blanket."

I unsaddled my horse and retrieved my saddle blanket. Wendy circled toward the trap. "When I say Go," Wendy commanded, "you cover his head with the blanket and hold him. I'll open the trap."

On Wendy's signal, I dropped the blanket. The small dog scarcely noticed. His pain had overwhelmed him. Wendy held open the trap as I lifted out his foot. We carried him on our horses to the ranch, then drove him to the veterinarian.

God answered our prayers and gave that little dog another chance at life. His recovery was almost complete. Only Wendy and I could see his slight limp.

When I heard that tiny dog wailing in pain, it touched a chord in my heart. I understood how pain can make you strike out even at those who want to help you. Sometimes I strike out at God, saying, "Why do I have to suffer with food addiction? Why didn't You give me a body and mind that can handle food?" In my pain I blame God, yet He is the One who can give me victory over my addiction.

Today I did like that little dog. I once again laid down my pain and said, "Lord, I can't fight it anymore. Please help." I began to feel the blanket of healing surrounding my heart and mind, bringing health and victory back into my life.

## Prayer

***Lord of healing, thank You for taking my pain.***

## Affirmation

My God gives me victory over the pain of addiction.

# *SOURCE OF COURAGE*

***Have I not commanded you? Be strong and courageous. Do not be terrified; do not be discouraged, for the Lord your God will be with you wherever you go (Joshua 1:9).***

My sixteen-year-old daughter chauffeured her little brother to 4-H registration so I could finish some work at home. When they bounced back through the door, both faces beamed with excitement.

"Mom!" my son yelled, "Sis joined 4-H too."

I was speechless with surprise.

"Yeah," she chimed in, "I signed up for rock rappelling." (My brows lifted in question.) "You know, mountain climbing."

"Oh my," I replied. "I'd never have the courage for that."

"Yes you would, Mom," she said. "You're braver than you think."

"Sure, Mom," my son agreed. "Remember how you learned to ride a horse even after you were bucked off and really scared?"

"How about the time Dad moved us to New York,"

my daughter added. "All you had was us and a street map to help you find your way around."

"Remember that time Dad was gone and we had the ice storm," my son reminded. "We didn't have electricity or phones for days. You didn't cry or nothing!"

I laughed and replied, "I think you need a different kind of courage for climbing mountains."

After the kids scurried away to bed, I remained for a while to think about what they had said. There are many kinds of courage, but only one main source for it. I vividly remembered praying my way through all the situations they had mentioned.

I need to draw on God's promise to be with me and to give me the courage to face defeats and disappointments. I need to turn to God instead of to food in times of stress. Food is not my source of comfort and courage; God is. He will support my sagging spirits in troubled times.

## Prayer

***God, thank You for Your promise to be with me wherever I go.***

## Affirmation

God is my source of courage.

# WINGS OF VICTORY

***We have escaped like a bird out of the fowler's snare; the snare has been broken, and we have escaped (Psalm 124:7).***

One spring morning I went into our garage, hunting for a hammer. As I searched the shelves near our wood-burning stove, I heard a scratching sound. I leaned toward the stove and listened closely.

*Sure enough, there is something in our stove! Oh, it's merely the wind coming down the chimney and blowing something unburned in there.*

Satisfied with my theory, I pulled on the door handle to take a peek. No sooner did I open the door than a tiny wren whizzed out right through the top of my hair! Further frightened by my shout of surprise, the wren frantically flew around the garage, trying to escape yet another prison.

Taking deep breaths in an attempt to calm my own pounding heart, I watched the bird flutter in panic from rafter to rafter.

*If only I could speak to him and show him the way out of the garage, but my words would only frighten him more.*

I inched over to the side door and quietly opened it. Turning off the garage light, I waited for him to go toward the daylight through the door. Time hung suspended as I waited for him to comprehend his escape route. Finally, he flew to freedom.

As I watched the wren disappear upward, I understood how he must have felt. I am like that bird in the stove—powerless to open the door to freedom from food addiction. I ask for help in a panic, blinded by the darkness of fear. First, God calms my fears, then opens the door to my freedom. He waits patiently until I understand and soar toward the light.

Today as I ate a fresh peach instead of peach pie, I felt the fresh air of freedom support my wings of victory.

## *Prayer*

***Lord, I'm not only escaping from food addiction, but also finding a clearer light of faith.***

## Affirmation

I'm soaring toward freedom from food addiction.

# A TREASURED JEWEL

***Do not be deceived: God cannot be mocked. A man reaps what he sows (Galatians 6:7).***

In 1972 my husband and I sank our life savings into starting our own business. We worked twelve- to sixteen-hour days, six days a week. I answered the phone, typed, filed, sorted, organized, cleaned toilets, and tried to corral two young children. (Money for a baby sitter simply didn't exist.)

After an exhausting day at the office, I still needed to do laundry and housework, buy groceries, and prepare meals. (Eating out, even at fast-food restaurants, was beyond our tight budget.) Next came baths for two rambunctious little ones, reading stories, and saying prayers.

One hot August evening, after a hectic day at work, I arrived home with two cross, hungry children. From intense fatigue and stress I collapsed in a chair in tears. I didn't see how I could manage one other task that day. At that moment my husband pulled into our driveway, bringing me a much-needed gift. For $15 he'd bought a dishwasher at a garage sale. He tinkered with it for a few hours, transforming it into a workable blessing.

I babied and cared for that dishwasher like a treasured jewel. In return, it hummed proficiently through load after load of dirty dishes.

I remembered the special care I gave that machine when I recently read a quote from Nancy Ryan, a nutritionist with the American Fitness Institute in Greenwich, Connecticut: "Treat your body as a machine, giving it only the best nutrients so it can perform to its fullest potential."

Am I sowing good nutrition in order to reap my "fullest potential"? When I eat a well-balanced diet and maintain a moderate exercise program, I reap a slender, healthy, energetic body.

***Lord, I promise today I will take care of my "treasured jewel"—good health.***

## Affirmation

Good nutrition equals good health.

# BAIL ME OUT

***It is for freedom that Christ has set us free. Stand firm, then, and do not let yourselves be burdened again by a yoke of slavery (Galatians 5:1).***

It was a typical morning service in our small rural church. The sun beamed a mosaic pattern of colors through the century-old stained-glass windows. The wooden pews squeaked as people settled down for the sermon.

Our pastor told us the story of a man who lived in the 1800s. He had a strong Christian faith and prayed about each decision he needed to make. One day, after praying with other Christian friends, he took a stand that caused his arrest.

As I listened to the story, I silently cheered the brave Christian man and felt proud of belonging to such a heritage. However, the pastor's next remark shocked me. "What would you do if I were thrown into jail?"

My immediate reaction was bewilderment. But across the aisle sat seventy-year-old Nettie. She instantly answered the pastor's question. "I'd bail ya out."

The pastor flashed Nettie a thankful grin, and the congregation chuckled. All of us who knew Nettie had no doubt she'd do exactly what she said.

The pastor continued the sermon, and I forgot the incident until later in the week. I had taken a stand on faith when I asked God to help me overcome compulsive overeating. That day, however, food temptations arrested my thoughts. In a panic, I prayed, "Jesus, bail me out before I binge!" He reminded me about one of the Overeaters Anonymous tools.

OA teaches us to use the telephone as a tool for calling another member when we need encouragement. I called for help. A prayer with an understanding friend supported my stand on faith. My friend reminded me that all I needed to do was be willing to turn over my food addiction to God. I knew that in my head, but my friend helped me remember it in my heart.

*God of freedom, thank You for sending me friends to "bail me out."*

## Affirmation

Friendship equals victory.

# *WITHOUT COMPLAINING*

***Do everything without complaining or arguing (Philippians 2:14).***

The complaints begin on the third or fourth day of restrictive eating. "If it's delicious, it has to be high in calories. I'll never get to eat anything that tastes good." Fantasies of eating unlimited amounts of calorie-rich foods follow.

The next stage is arguing. A small scrimmage begins it: "One small bite isn't going to make any difference." The artillery moves in as I clear the dinner table: "No use saving that little dab of food." My thrifty conscience won't allow me to throw the food away; I become a human garbage disposal.

Next come the big guns and final surrender: "Well, I've eaten this much; I might as well have cake and ice cream too."

The vicious cycle begins with a negative mind game of complaining and arguing.

When Christian ideas entered the world, one of the most startling concepts was the Christian's positive approach to life. This differed drastically from the heathen religions based on fear and fate.

Paul taught how the mind can be used to improve human beings. He told us to renew our minds (see Romans 12:2), to have a new attitude (see Ephesians 4:24), and to serve in a new way (see Romans 7:6).

I will follow His teachings to become a new creation. I will fill my mind with positive thoughts to improve my appearance and health.

I will imagine comfortable breathing and easy movement in my clothes. I'll picture in my mind getting clothes altered to a smaller size. I'll think about how delightful it will feel to see my thinner body in the mirror and to hear people tell me how nice I look. I will present a positive appearance for a positive faith.

***Lord Jesus, thank You for teaching me how to use my mind in a positive way.***

## Affirmation

I am a positive-minded Christian.



7—T.B.M.

# *THE ACTION KEY*

***If you, then, though you are evil, know how to give good gifts to your children, how much more will your Father in heaven give good gifts to those who ask him! Matthew 7:11 (NIV)***

When we first moved to our ranch, I didn't realize what it would mean to be 150 miles from the nearest shopping center. I suffered through the pain of "shopping center withdrawal!" When I felt I could bear it no more, I discovered a computer program that allowed me to shop from my home. Using it, I had access to anything I could ever think about wanting.

I browse through computer screen after computer screen, all showing merchandise in bright colors with clever graphics. I look at the pictures, read the descriptions and decide what I want. Once I decide, I simply move my cursor to the word ACTION and push that key. A few days later the merchandise is delivered to my door.

Today, while I tried to locate a special hoe on the gardening screen, I thought how great it would be if God had a computer program like this. If I felt I needed healing, all I would have to do is call up the "health screen" and push the ACTION key.

Wouldn't it be great if He had a screen for: money, success, . . . freedom from food abuse?

With thoughts of a compulsive overeating screen, I snapped back to reality. Often my prayers treat God as if He is running a gigantic shopping center for prayer requests. When the Bible talks about God giving us gifts, it isn't talking about merchandise and fantasies.

God does give victory in my prayer life, but I'm the one who runs the computer screens and the one to push the ACTION key. I need to be willing to accept His help. It's hard to be willing to hit the ACTION key for freedom from food abuse. I want to be thin, healthy and free, but I don't want to give up sweets or refined carbohydrates. I'm afraid of feeling hungry. I take a step toward abstinence by praying for God's Spirit of courage.

During the last few days, I asked God to help me abstain from sweets. He met me more than halfway with His power. He gave me unbelievable victory.

Abstinence for me is one "screen" at a time with God helping me push the ACTION key.

## *Prayer*

***Lord of hope, thank You for meeting me more than halfway down the path to victory.***

## Affirmation

When I take ACTION, God delivers the victory.

# *JULIE'S WINDOW*

***Because of God's great kindness, Jesus tasted death for everyone in all the world (Hebrews 2:9, TLB).***

Day after day as I sit at my desk working, my miniature dachshund, Julie, sits in the recliner by the picture window. She props her front feet up on the chair arm so she can see out the window. Hour after hour, she sits there, keeping vigilant watch. I can't see anything outside the window but sagebrush, rocks, and an occasional bird. What does she see outside my office window that I can't see? Am I missing a whole world of activity?

During years of suffering from low self-esteem, I hid from the outside world and fed my loneliness by overeating. My vision of the outside world became blurred. For a time, I even stopped looking out my window at life. I reasoned that if I didn't go out or even glance outside, I'd have fewer chances of being hurt. Rather than risk rejection, I hid.

I found that isolation tactics didn't stop the hurts.

They were only a trade-off for loneliness.

When I became a Christian, I felt the fulfillment of acceptance. I reasoned, "If God accepts me, then I must accept myself." Yet years of putting myself down made self-acceptance nearly impossible.

One Easter Sunday our minister said, "If you were the only sinner in the world, Christ would have died just for you." I realized that if God saw me as that valuable, it was wrong for me to belittle His sacrifice for me. As I sang about Christ's triumph over His foe—death—I knew He gladly gave me the power to triumph over my foe—low self-esteem.

God gave me Julie to guide my first step outside. Whenever neighbors arrive with a dog in the back of their pickup truck, Julie is the first one out the door, anxious to get acquainted. Sometimes the other dog is friendly, and they play chase or wrestle around in the yard. Once in a while, the other dog is unfriendly and growls and nips at her. In spite of occasional encounters with unfriendly dogs, she eagerly races out the door to meet the next visiting dog.

With my growing trust in God, I now have courage to step out that door and risk making friends. I no longer sit inside, overeating to comfort my loneliness. Each new friendship, each deepening relationship, is a victorious step empowered by my conquering Lord.

*I praise You, Lord, for helping me triumph over low self-esteem.*

## Affirmation

Risking friendships reduces hunger.

# SELF-LOVE

***We know and rely on the love God has for us. God is love. Whoever lives in love lives in God, and God in him (1 John 4:16).***

"Yes, love is the magic key of life—not to get what we want but to become what we ought to be," says Eileen Guder, the prominent author of several inspirational books.

Psychologists believe people often overeat from a lack of self-love. They keep trying to feed an insatiable hunger.

Sometimes I search for just the right food to satisfy a special hunger. I eat something sweet, but it doesn't satisfy me. Then I try something salty. No, that isn't quite it. Maybe something crunchy or chewy or spicy will work. On and on the cycle goes, but I never find the perfect food.

When I offer some yummy food I've just cooked to a friend who declines because she "isn't hungry," I reply, "What does hunger have to do with it?" We both laugh, but inside I know it isn't funny.

There is no more humor in being overweight than in

having an ulcer. The latter is a disease of the body; the former a dis-ease of the soul.

To silence my inner cries for food, I must believe God loves me. If God loves me, then I'm worthy of love, and it's OK to love myself. Hating myself or feeling unworthy of love hasn't improved me any—it's only made me fat and unhappy. It's time I tried loving myself into what I ought to be and, deep below the physical cravings, what I truly want to be. To learn to love, I must go to the source of love, which is God. His Spirit will comfort me, filling the void inside me that I fail to satisfy with food.

## *Prayer*

***Father, fill me with Your perfect love.***

## Affirmation

I am a child of God. I am worthy of love.

# AWARENESS

***Do you not know that your body is a temple of the Holy Spirit, who is in you, whom you have received from God? You are not your own; you were bought at a price. Therefore honor God with your body (1 Corinthians 6:19, 20).***

A busy week slipped by without time to run upstairs to check my ten-year-old son's room. When I opened his bedroom door on Friday morning, my hand flew to my nose! The smell of sour milk, sweaty socks, and a dirty hamster cage filled the room. Filthy clothes, wadded-up school papers, and smashed aluminum cans covered the floor. The night stand held a glass of curdled milk and a bowl of something greenish-gray growing in it.

As I snapped a dirty T-shirt off his mirror, my hand halted in midair. My reflection, from neck to knees, gleamed before me. When had my body, the temple of the Holy Spirit, become so distorted by rolls of fat? My "temple" resembled my son's room—a body filled with the garbage of junk food, sweets, leftovers from the kids' plates, and a steady procession of bites and snacks.

The anger I'd felt about my son's room now transferred to my body. How had I been so unaware of my behavior? Who was in control? God? My mind? My body! Even more, what was I going to do about it?

*Time to clean house—and not just my son's room,* I decided. *Time to get rid of the garbage I'd been shoving into my body.* I wanted a clean, healthy dwelling place for God's Spirit.

## *Prayer*

***Lord, thank You for making me aware of what I've been doing to my body and health. Show me how to clean Your temple.***

## Affirmation

Today I will be aware of what I put into my body.

# MATURE TASTE BUDS

***Anyone who lives on milk, being still an infant, is not acquainted with the teaching about righteousness. But solid food is for the mature, who by constant use have trained themselves to distinguish good from evil (Hebrews 5:13, 14).***

When our son was six months old, I placed him on a blanket in our front yard. He tried eating rocks and weeds. When he began crawling, he found a can of dirt in his older sister's bedroom closet and gulped down half the contents. (His sister couldn't explain how the can of dirt got there or why.)

Once he began to walk, he left an eating trail: tooth marks in a bar of soap, fingerprints on a stick of butter, and dog food missing from the bowl while the dog visited the veterinarian.

He never suffered any ill effects from his foraging, but I maintained a round-the-clock vigil to eliminate the possibility.

One morning as I stuffed clothes into the washer, he discovered a bottle of bleach. (How his tiny fingers removed the lid remains a mystery.) I turned from the machine the moment the bleach bottle touched his lips and snatched it out of his hands before a drop of liquid flowed out. God gave us both a second chance.

Today our son is six feet tall, slender, and healthy. He decided somewhere along the way that he preferred salads, potatoes, and Mom's homemade bread. His taste buds grew up.

Things I eat, such as overprocessed fast foods, are as nutritious for me as rocks and dirt. High-fat and sugary foods are nearly as dangerous to my body as bleach. My taste buds need to grow up.

As I draw closer to God, seeking His help to mature my eating habits, I find myself growing in my spiritual life as well. I'm learning to open my heart and mind to His Spirit. I'm developing obedience and trust.

*Father, help me distinguish good from evil in my spiritual life and nutritious from nonnutritious in my eating behavior.*

## Affirmation

My eating behavior is mature.

# *PRAYER*

***Therefore I tell you, whatever you ask for in prayer, believe that you have received it, and it will be yours (Mark 11:24).***

Sticking with my proper diet and exercise plan produced visible results. Several people pleaded for my secret. "Prayer," I confessed. I felt a tiny bit smug at being such a great witness. Then the test came.

I'd prepared a glorious Easter dinner for company. Like my meal, my control was superb. I'd even passed on my favorite, strawberry cheesecake.

After eating, we all retreated downstairs to the family room to watch a TV special. I returned upstairs, alone, to brew a hot drink. As I drew the water from the tap, the cheesecake started calling to me through the refrigerator door, "Come on, have a piece. With the TV noise, no one will hear you." My mind flashed dozens of flimsy reasons why it was permissible, such as "I can still be a good witness if no one sees me indulge."

I picked up a fork and headed toward the dessert. The moment I opened the refrigerator door, I heard a man on TV proclaim, "Get thee behind me, Satan!" The same instant, that cheesecake transformed into an evil, jeering face.

I slammed the refrigerator door and slipped the clean fork back into the silverware drawer. After I placed the teakettle on the stove, I hurried back downstairs. I asked my daughter to bring the hot drinks after the water had time to heat.

Later that night, as I lay in bed, I wondered about that voice I'd heard. Had it really been on TV? I never had the nerve to ask my family.

I'd prayed to hear God's guidance in my proper eating plan. Why was I startled when He answered my prayers?

## Prayer

***Heavenly Father, I am dedicated to making my body-temple clean and healthy for Your Holy Spirit. Thank You for answering my prayers.***

## Affirmation

God answers prayers (sometimes with a sense of humor).

# SPIRITUAL FOOD

***In all these things we are more than conquerors through him who loved us (Romans 8:37).***

My goal for the past three springs has been to hike up Spud Creek and make the full loop back home. The first half of the trail climbs steeply upward.

The first year I tried it, I was completely organized. I wore heavy hiking boots, jeans, and a heavy sweater. In a backpack, I stuffed a jacket, a fat lunch, a large canteen of water, snakebite kit, compass, altimeter, extra bandanna, a waterproof Walkman with assorted tapes, a pack of tissues, lip balm, camera, and extra film. I strapped on my pedometer and began my climb.

Halfway up, my feet ached, my knees quivered, and I gasped for breath. I knew I couldn't make the loop with my heavy load, and I feared abandoning it along the trail. Convinced it couldn't be done—at least not by me—I gave up and returned home.

The second spring, I came up with a plan to do the impossible. I wore lighter hiking boots, jeans, and a light sweater. I strapped on a fanny-pack filled with a canteen of water, a granola bar, a few tissues, and lip balm. I made it almost to the top before turning back.

The third spring, I tried a little different approach. For three weeks, I hiked around the ranch for an hour each day. Then I hung a small canteen of water around my neck, stuffed a tissue into my pocket, and began my climb. I conquered the summit and enjoyed the sensation of personal achievement.

Climbing that summit is a lot like overcoming food addiction. I learned to lighten my load to aid my progress. As it says in Harper/Hazelden's book, *Food for Thought*, "We gradually learn that eating less physical food enables us to make more spiritual progress."

Spiritual food satisfies the hunger I foolishly tried to appease with excess physical food. Practicing abstinence from overeating lightens my physical burden and aids my spiritual progress.

I'm practicing for my climb each day when I turn my food choices and my life over to God's control. He feeds my body with proper nutrition and my soul with a closer relationship with Him.

With God as my source of energy, I am conquering my summit toward freedom from food abuse. With each triumphant step, I feel the wind of His Holy Spirit carrying me closer to Him.

8—T.B.M.

## *Prayer*

***Triumphant Lord, thank You for Your spiritual food of true fulfillment.***

## Affirmation

Spiritual food feeds my true hunger.

# *FEEL THE BRAKES*

***Let us not be like others, who are asleep, but let us be alert and self-controlled (1 Thessalonians 5:6).***

After my foot surgery, I prepared myself for the three days I would be unable to walk. Lounging on the couch with James Michener's latest bestseller, my sore foot propped on a pillow, I was ready to endure my confinement with pleasure.

As I finished the first page, my husband dashed into the living room. "Honey, you've got to meet the letter carrier with this deposit. I just got a call that we have cattle up Mule Creek."

"I can't drive! My foot's still numb."

"Oh, you can drive one mile to the mailbox. This deposit has to be in today's mail, and I have to get those cows before a car hits one of 'em." Without waiting for further discussion, he left.

I managed to meet the mailman, then headed back home. To eliminate walking a few extra steps, I decided to pull up close to the house. I pushed on the brake, but the car didn't stop! Before I realized it only *felt* as if I were pushing on the brake, I'd crashed the car into the house!

Knees shaking, foot throbbing, I crawled out of the car to check the damage. The car showed no dents or scratches, but the wood on the house was splintered.

When my husband arrived home that evening, I greeted him with a strong defense. "Did you see what *you* caused?"

"Me? What?"

"You made me run into the house!"

"How could you hit a house? Didn't you see it?" he replied with a grin tickling the corner of his mouth.

Hesitating for a moment between anger and humor, I went with the laughter. "Yes, I saw the house, but it was in my way, so I decided to plow through it."

"Sounds normal," my husband said, chuckling. "I guess a nail and a dab of paint will fix it."

The grain of truth hidden inside the exaggeration applied to other areas of my life. Many times I see problems as obstacles in my path that I need to "plow through." Then, when I crash, I don't want to take the blame.

No one forced me to become overweight; I did it all by myself. Instead of trying to mindlessly plow through the problems of weight loss, I need to maintain an awareness of what I'm doing. A large portion of my eating is unconscious. I eat while I read, watch TV, or get involved in deep discussions. Like my numb foot, I can't feel the brakes until I'm stuffed.

Today, I will concentrate on the taste, texture, and aroma of food. I will be alert to my body's signals that it has had enough to eat.

## *Prayer*

***Keep me alert, Lord, and self-controlled.***

## Affirmation

I am conscious of what I'm eating.

# OPEN DOORS

***Everyone who asks receives; he who seeks finds; and to him who knocks, the door will be opened (Luke 11:10).***

My miniature dachshund is starting to get old and is sometimes impatient with me. When she was a puppy, she learned to scratch on the door when she wanted in or out. If she was outside, she scratched once or twice, then waited quietly for me to open the door. If I didn't hear her, she'd scratch again, then peek in the low window. If I still didn't hear, she'd lie on the porch, patiently waiting until I remembered her.

That is no longer her habit. If I don't open the door instantly, she stands in the center of the porch, barking with such force it makes her bounce on all four paws. This continues until I meet her demands. When I open the door, she charges across the porch, tears through the doorway, and races on across the living room. There she slides to a stop, tucking her tiny hind legs in toward her belly like a cutting horse. Then she turns and smiles at me. (I haven't decided whether it's a "thank you" smile or an "I knew I could make you do it" smile.)

When I respond to her impatient demands and open the door, I love watching her race into the house. Today when I held the door, I wondered how many times I've "barked" at God, asking Him to open doors for me. "Lord, open the doors to weight loss for me," I'd plead. "Show me how to eat correctly. Lead me to the proper eating habits." Then when the Lord opened the door for me, I merely stood in the center of the porch, eyes squeezed shut, continuing to bark to be let in.

## Prayer

***Lord, help me to open my eyes and see Your open doors to better eating habits. Give me the courage to race through them to a healthier lifestyle.***

## Affirmation

I'm alert to God's open doors.

# DAVID

***God did not give us a spirit of timidity, but a spirit of power, of love and of self-discipline (2 Timothy 1:7).***

A week after school started, the kindergarten teacher introduced me to one of her students. "This is David. He would like to be in your reading class."

David was a handsome boy, taller than some of my second graders. The other students easily accepted him.

No one realized he'd taught himself to read until he was tested for kindergarten. He read as well as my best students. He also understood math concepts that most sixth graders struggle with.

David was brilliant. He learned his lessons quickly and never created a disturbance. It was hard to remember he was only five years old.

One day he completed his assignment early and wanted to try a fun activity. I showed him a picture he could color and cut out on the crooked lines to make a puzzle.

Five minutes later I found David slumped over his desk crying. Between sobs he told me, "I don't . . . know how . . . to use scissors."

When he calmed down, I let him help a slower reading student with his assignment. Then that student taught David how to use a pair of scissors.

David became upset with himself when he could not maintain his high level of achievement in *all* areas of his life. He had not yet learned about the uneven development of skills.

My own skills are also unevenly developed. I have the self-discipline to get out of bed when the alarm goes off, but not to get through the checkout counter without buying a candy bar. I carefully budget my money for bills, but eat handful after handful of peanuts without a thought. I finish my work before I play, but rarely pass on a serving of coconut-cream pie. Like David, I have a loving Teacher to wipe my tears of failure and redirect my learning.

## Prayer

***Lord, help me to have Your spirit of self-discipline more evenly developed in my personality.***

## Affirmation

God gives me the power to develop self-control.

# FREEDOM

***You, my brothers, were called to be free. But do not use your freedom to indulge the sinful nature; rather, serve one another in love (Galatians 5:13).***

The only route to my doctor's office is over 8,000-foot Galena Summit. The drive last February was on solid, snow-packed roads. Not once during the trip did the gray pavement peek through the glaring snow.

I released a deep sigh of relief when I finally left the summit behind me and drove into town. I told myself the reason the street looked black was that my eyes were used to staring at the bright snow. I'd never heard of "black ice."

Glancing at my watch, I pulled away from the intersection. With plenty of time to make my appointment, I loosened my grip on the steering wheel and relaxed.

I wasn't disturbed when my rear tires slowly slid sideways. I merely removed my foot from the accelerator and waited for the car to stop. Five seconds later my car was buried upside down in a snowdrift. Buckled in my seat belt, I hung, unhurt, in space. My predominant thought was freedom. I unsnapped my belt and fell against the steering wheel. Seeing nothing but snow packed against every window, I suppressed the panic that wanted to kick through the windows to freedom. Muffled voices from outside my white sepulcher gave me enough control to wait for my rescue.

Losing my freedom of movement, even for that short period of time, was suffocating and frightening. Each time I give in to compulsive overeating, I lose my freedom of choice. Eating anything, anytime, in any amount imprisons me. I'm not serving myself or anyone else. Freedom from food is exercising the choice not to over-indulge.

## *Prayer*

***Thank You, Lord, for the freedom I have in You.***

## Affirmation

With Christ as my help, I choose freedom from my bondage to food.

# *REJECTED CALF*

***Those who live according to the sinful nature have their minds set on what that nature desires; but those who live in accordance with the Spirit have their minds set on what the Spirit desires (Romans 8:5).***

One of our first-year heifers had her calf late at night in the pouring rain. Unlike most cows, she didn't lick her baby clean or nudge it to stand and nurse.

The newborn calf called feebly, but the mother ignored him. She wanted nothing to do with the troublesome creature. Despite the lack of help, the calf managed a wobbly standing position. The sucking instinct pushed him toward his mother, but she backed off a few feet, lowered her head, and charged him. He tumbled away. The scene was repeated before we could intervene.

We lured the heifer into a barn stall and tied her in place. Now she could no longer charge her calf, but she kicked him each time he tried to nurse.

My neighbor suggested, "If you can get her to let him nurse once, she might accept him."

After we tied the cow's legs together so she couldn't kick, the calf nursed and gained some strength. But as soon as we turned the cow loose, she charged her calf again.

Sometimes nature goes against God's perfect plan. We had no control over that heifer's mothering instincts and had to give the calf to another cow.

Compulsive overeating is not God's perfect plan for me either. Yet I don't know why I'm compelled to overeat any more than I know why that cow disowned her calf. I know that trying to force myself to stop food abuse is no more successful than trying to force that cow to let her baby nurse. Unlike that cow, I have more to rely on than damaged instincts.

Just for today, I can accept God's healing power to abstain from overeating. I can't control tomorrow or next week; but for these twenty-four hours, I can accept God's offered victory over my damaged instincts.

***Thank You, Lord, for giving me victory today.***

## Affirmation

God heals my damaged instincts.

# PATIENCE

***The Lord longs to be gracious to you; he rises to show you compassion. For the Lord is a God of justice. Blessed are all who wait for him! (Isaiah 30:18).***

When it's time to prepare dinner, I page through my microwave cookbook for ideas. If the recipe requires more than ten minutes, I skip it for a quicker one.

I know I'm a product of my culture; I'm programmed for instant results. Along with the burdens of haste, I add the demands of achievement. I must be constantly doing, getting, and accomplishing. My definition of a "good day" is a productive day. I tell myself, today I will read twenty-five verses of Scripture, prepare three low-calorie meals, run sixteen errands, make seven phone calls, bake three loaves of whole-wheat bread, wash ten windows, and run the vacuum in three rooms.

My list is made out; my pencil is ready to mark off my accomplishments. Number one is reading Scripture. I perch on the edge of a chair, cranking up my speed-reading skills. Opening my Bible to Psalm 27:14 I read, "Wait for the Lord. . . ." *Wait! I don't have time for that.*

I flip over a few pages to Psalm 37:7. "Be still before the Lord and wait patiently for him. . . ." *That's Old Testament thought; I'd better read from the New Testament.* I turn to Romans 8:25. "If we hope for what we do not yet have, we wait for it patiently." *Are you trying to get a point across to me, Lord?*

The Lord is saying that I not only need to wait, but I also need to wait patiently. But I want my prayers answered *now.* I want my excess weight gone *today.* I want to be free from compulsive eating habits *yesterday!* How can I wait patiently in an impatient world?

How can I not wait? Even though God is always there for me to come to, He didn't put me in charge of His time schedule for answered prayers. He waited for me to accept His gift of salvation. He waited patiently for me to study and learn His precepts. He waits for me to become quiet and listen to His guiding Spirit.

***Lord, help me still my mind and heart to receive Your patient work in me.***

## Affirmation

"I will wait for the Lord" (Isaiah 8:17).